WORLD WAR II 1　　　　　5

ROOSEVELT
AND THE AMERICANS AT WAR

ROBIN CROSS

FRANKLIN WATTS
London · New York · Toronto · Sydney

AN UN-AMERICAN CHILDHOOD

Franklin Delano Roosevelt was born on the Hudson River estate of Springwood in upstate New York on 30 January 1882, the only son of James and Sara Delano Roosevelt. It was a time when half the population of the United States was on the move. Great tracts of the West – including the territories of Arizona and New Mexico, the Dakotas, Oklahoma, Utah and Idaho, Washington, Wyoming and Montana – were waiting to be claimed by land-hungry homesteaders. As the railways drove westwards across the great plains, ramshackle towns mushroomed in their wake, with tribes of Indians encamped outside them in their teepees.

Franklin Roosevelt photographed with his mother Sara in 1893. She had a considerable influence over her son throughout her life.

The Springwood estate, family home of the Roosevelts, was so far removed from the rip-roaring cow-towns of the West or the slums of New York's Lower East Side that it might have been on a different planet. If there was such a thing as an American aristocracy then the Roosevelts would have been among them. The family claimed descent from the original 17th century Dutch settlers of New York, and by the early 19th century were comfortably established as wealthy landowners in the beautiful Hudson Valley. Their neighbours, the Vanderbilts, were richer but were regarded as mere upstarts, their invitations to dinner politely declined.

The Roosevelts' genteel style drew on European rather than American models. English cattle, not Texas longhorns, grazed on James Roosevelt's estate. His tweed suits came from a tailor in Edinburgh, his shoes from Peal's of London, shoemakers to the Royal Family. The Roosevelts took frequent overseas trips to visit the spas of Europe. In Paris in 1890 James Roosevelt took his son Franklin to the top of the recently completed Eiffel Tower.

Franklin's was a very un-American childhood, bathed in the uncritical love of his parents and insulated from anxiety by wealth and property. From the age of five he was dressed in the Murray kilt, a Scottish clan with which the Roosevelt family claimed a distant connection. He was taught French and German by private tutors, and on his 14th birthday his father presented him with a 21-ft yacht, complete with a tiny cabin containing two bunks and an oil stove.

That year he arrived at Groton School in Massachusetts, a prestigious private school, in the family's private rail car. At Groton, Franklin slipped easily into the active and competitive life of the school. He was not academically outstanding but he shone in school debates. Nor was he physically robust, but he tested his courage in the Groton "high kick", an eccentric and dangerous game in which the contestants attempted to kick a tin pan suspended from the ceiling. At his first attempt Franklin won the Class III kick, reaching seven feet and three and a half inches.

At this impressionable stage in his life Franklin fell under the spell of a distant relative, his fifth cousin Theodore Roosevelt, then the Police Commissioner of New York City and soon to become Assistant Secretary of the Navy. "Cousin Theodore" was everything that Franklin's politely ineffectual father James was not: an intellectual and a man of action who could rope a steer as well as any cowboy on the range. He possessed boundless energy and strong political convictions. At Groton the students were urged to make careers in politics and public service.

Theodore Roosevelt was living proof that a gentleman could succeed in political service. The post of Assistant Secretary of the Navy quickly proved too confining for a man of such restless energy, and when war broke out with Spain in 1898 he organised the Rough Riders and fought his way to glory in a famous charge up San Juan Hill. On his return from war he was elected governor of New York, where he launched a fierce anti-corruption campaign. Indeed, so successful

"Cousin Teddy" – Theodore Roosevelt, who became president of the United States. Much of FDR's early political career was a conscious attempt to emulate the achievements of his distinguished cousin.

was Roosevelt's drive against corruption that the threatened city bosses rid themselves of him by securing his nomination as President William McKinley's running mate in the election of 1900. In September 1901, McKinley was assassinated by an anarchist and, at the age of 42, Theodore Roosevelt found himself elevated to the presidency. "Cousin Teddy" had now set Franklin Roosevelt another goal at which to aim – the highest office in the United States.

Franklin's connection with his famous cousin was strengthened during his final year as a student at Harvard University, when he became engaged to Theodore Roosevelt's niece, Eleanor Roosevelt. Three years younger than Franklin, she was a woman with a strong personality already marked by her social work among the poor in New York City. They were married on 17 March 1905, while Franklin was studying at the Columbia University School of Law. Franklin Roosevelt's legal career was brief and undistinguished. In 1907 he was taken on as a clerk in the prestigious Wall Street firm of Carter, Ledyard and Milburn. He adopted an attitude of detachment to the legal profession; his mind was already on bigger things – entering politics. In 1945 Grenville Clark, a former Harvard classmate and fellow clerk on Wall Street, recalled a conversation of 1907: "We were a small group with desks together in one large room, and in our leisure hours naturally fell into discussions of our hopes and ambitions. I remember him saying with engaging frankness that he wasn't going to practise law forever, that he intended to run for office at the first opportunity, and that he wanted to be and thought he had a good chance to be president. I remember he described . . . the steps which he thought could lead to this goal. They were: first, a seat in the State Assembly, then an appointment as Assistant Secretary of the Navy . . . and finally the Governorship of New York." With the exception of the very first step, this was a remarkably accurate forecast of the future president's political career.

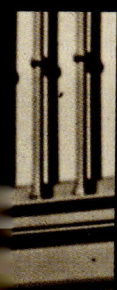

ENTRY INTO POLITICS

Theodore Roosevelt was a Republican, but when Franklin took the political plunge in 1910 it was as a member of the Democratic Party. Democratic Party leaders in Dutchess County, in upstate New York, persuaded him to run in an apparently hopeless campaign for the state Senate. Roosevelt threw himself into the rough and tumble of electioneering with all the energy and limitless confidence of youth. In his first lesson in the demands of electoral politics he learned how to drop the manners of the son of the "squire of Springwood" and address the voters as equals. He criss-crossed his district in an automobile – a daring innovation in those "horse and buggy" days – addressing as many as seven meetings a day.

On the stump: Roosevelt running for the New York state Senate in 1910, a campaign which marked his entry into politics.

Doubtless his famous name was no handicap for him at the polls, but 1910 was a good year for the Democrats, who took control of both houses in New York state and the House of Representatives in Washington DC. Thus it was that in the 26th senatorial district of New York a new young man in politics, Franklin Roosevelt, beat his Republican opponent John Schlosser by 15,708 votes to 14,568, ending 25 years of Republican rule.

Roosevelt's spell in the New York Senate gave him his first insight into political tactics and the handling of people. He became a champion of the upstate farmers, and also an advocate of nature conservation, but at this stage in his career he showed little interest in wider issues of social reform, particularly the campaign to improve working conditions and shorten working hours. An attack of typhoid fever did not stop Roosevelt from participating in the 1912 campaign, and he was re-elected to the state Senate.

Navy days

In 1911 Roosevelt was an early recruit to Woodrow Wilson's campaign to win the Democratic nomination for the presidency. Wilson won the nomination for the 1912 presidential race and, with Theodore Roosevelt running as a third-party, secured the presidency. In March 1913 Roosevelt received his reward, the post of Assistant Secretary of the Navy, the job Theodore had left in order to fight in the Spanish-American War. Roosevelt's job was to look after the day-to-day running of the Navy Department, which was a major employer of labour in the Navy Yards. He earned the tag of "the spark plug" who got things done.

In August 1914 war broke out in Europe, with Britain, France and Russia (the Allies) fighting Germany and Austria-Hungary. Roosevelt quickly became one of the most pro-Allied members of Wilson's administration, which was committed to keeping America out of the war. When Wilson narrowly won a second term as president in November 1916, the Democrats' slogan had been "He kept us out of the war." But unrestricted German submarine warfare pulled the United States into World War I. On 31 January 1917 Germany announced that all shipping, including neutral, would be sunk on sight by its U-boats in the war zone of the eastern Atlantic. On 2 February, Wilson broke off relations with Germany. The U-boats immediately began sinking American ships. Shortly afterwards, American newspapers revealed a German scheme, outlined in the "Zimmerman telegram", to help Mexico recover New Mexico. Reluctantly, Woodrow Wilson declared war on Germany on 6 April 1917.

America's entry into the war brought limitless resources to the Allied side, but they had to be mobilised. The government moved in to regulate every economic activity connected with the war. The war provided a new outlet for Roosevelt's energy. American naval activity was confined to the transport and protection of troops, the convoying of supply vessels and the hunting of U-boats. However, before the war ended in November 1918, Roosevelt launched one major project, a 390-km mine barrier across the North Sea, which Admiral William S Sims, commander of US naval operations in the Atlantic, described as "one of the wonders of the war". This was a slight exaggeration. The barrier failed to seal off the U-boats' exit to the Atlantic and, at most, sunk only six submarines. At a cost of $80 million this came out at about $13 million a submarine.

In July 1918 Roosevelt visited Europe and the war fronts. With almost schoolboyish enthusiasm, he revelled in the sights and sounds of the battlefield, although his aides kept him at a discreetly safe distance from danger.

Roosevelt emerged from the war with a reputation as an energetic "can do" administrator, but there was uncertainty about his trustworthiness. Doubts about Roosevelt's judgement were raised in his handling of an investigation into a homosexual ring at the Naval Training Center in Newport. Roosevelt authorised the employment of a small undercover unit, attached to his own office, to entrap homosexual sailors. A court of inquiry was convened at which Roosevelt denied all knowledge of the entrapment. His denials failed to convince the majority on the court, whose report, published in March 1921, candidly accused him of lying under oath.

The lean years

By the time the court of inquiry's damaging report appeared, Roosevelt's political career had suffered a more damaging setback. After a long deadlock at the 1920 Democratic Convention, the colourless James M Cox, a former governor of Ohio and not a Wilson supporter, was chosen to head the Democratic ticket for the 1920 election. To give the ticket balance, Roosevelt was nominated for the vice presidency.

The election turned into a referendum on the League of Nations, the international association of nations formed after World War I to preserve world peace. Wilson had ensured that the Democrats were committed to this very unpopular policy. There was a landslide for the Republican ticket, Warren Harding and Calvin Coolidge, who had appealed for a "return to normalcy". Americans had little time for high-minded schemes to promote international co-operation.

A rare campaign badge from the 1920 election campaign when James M Cox and FDR ran unsuccessfully against their Republican opponents, Warren Harding and Calvin Coolidge.

FDR delivering the nomination speech for Governor Al Smith at the 1924 Democratic Convention. This was FDR's first step back into big-time politics. The speech demonstrated that his political future was not affected by his inability to walk. FDR emerged from the experience of polio as a more mature and thoughtful man, no longer a playboy but a formidable politician.

Roosevelt had to settle for a different kind of vice presidency in the New York office of the Fidelity and Deposit Company of Maryland. Then, in August 1921, while he was on vacation on Campobello Island, New Brunswick, a major event utterly transformed his life.

He was stricken by polio, probably contracting the virus while swimming in a stagnant pool. He was left unable to walk unaided. Now he was dependent on a helping hand for even the most trivial daily tasks. This might have finished a lesser man, but it was the making of Roosevelt. As he fought unsuccessfully to regain the use of his legs, he changed both physically and mentally. His formerly slim torso strengthened and swelled out to compensate for the wasted limbs painfully shackled in metal braces which had to be locked and unlocked as he moved about. His jutting chin, jauntily tilted head, dazzling smile and bone-crushing handshake combined to give the impression that he had conquered his disability.

Roosevelt's wife Eleanor and his advisers realised that it was essential for his recovery that he remain active in his career and in politics. By now, however, his marriage had undergone a critical change. In September 1918 Eleanor had learned that her husband had been having a love affair with her social secretary, Lucy Mercer. The couple discussed divorce, but this would have wrecked Roosevelt's political hopes, so they decided to remain together. Roosevelt continued to have discreet affairs with a number of mistresses. However, Eleanor remained loyal to her husband and to his ambitions. In the mid-1920s, while he was concentrating on physical recovery, Eleanor began to devote an increasing amount of her time to liberal causes, particularly to the advancement of American blacks. The immediate result of Roosevelt's paralysis was to take him out of direct involvement in politics. This proved to be a blessing at a time when the Democratic Party's fortunes were at a low ebb.

The road back
In 1928 the years of enforced political exile came to an end. Roosevelt accepted nomination as governor of New York and won. His health had stood up well to the demands of the campaign, and once in office, Roosevelt began to build the power base from which to launch a bid for the presidency.

Roosevelt served two successive terms as governor, during which he developed many of the qualities he would need in higher office.

Throughout Roosevelt's second term as governor no problem was more pressing than that of the Great Depression. The 1920s had been a time of unparalleled economic prosperity in the United States, although not all Americans had enjoyed an equal share of the fruits of the boom. Then, in October 1929, the collapse of the New York stock market heralded a savage economic depression which brought the United States face to face with its biggest crisis since the Civil War of the 1860s.

Between 1929 and 1933 as many as 10,000 banks across the United States closed their doors in the bank failures: millions of people lost all their savings, factories slashed production, construction virtually ceased, and foreign trade slumped by two-thirds. Unemployment rose remorselessly. By 1933 the number of jobless had risen to between 12 and 15 million – nobody could keep an accurate count. In a country of some 120 million people, over 40 million were either unemployed or members of a family in which the principal breadwinner was jobless.

The Depression dealt a massive and potentially fatal blow to the cherished American belief in individualism and self-reliance. One believer, however, remained unmoved. President Herbert Hoover was an orphan who had become a self-made millionaire; he considered that "a man who has not made a million dollars by the time he is forty is not worth much." Millions of his fellow-Americans now found even a single dollar beyond their reach, but the president believed first and foremost in letting the Depression correct itself. But the Depression did not correct itself. It was not until 1932 that Hoover decided to intervene. The Reconstruction Finance Corporation was established to provide government funds for public works. To support farm prices, the Federal Farm Board purchased huge quantities of wheat and cotton. However, what was given with one hand was taken away with the other. Heavy cuts in state and local aid offset the modest success of the Reconstruction Finance Corporation.

As the Depression bit deeper, Roosevelt acted to mobilise the machinery of the state government to aid the economy. In the autumn of 1931 Roosevelt presided over the establishment in New York of the Temporary Emergency Relief Agency, which

Unemployed men queue at a Chicago soup kitchen set up in 1930 by the gangster Al Capone.

represented the first concrete step taken by any state in the United States to alleviate unemployment by direct government action. Increasingly, Roosevelt was being talked about as the most likely Democratic presidential nominee for 1932. While denying any personal desire to be president, he

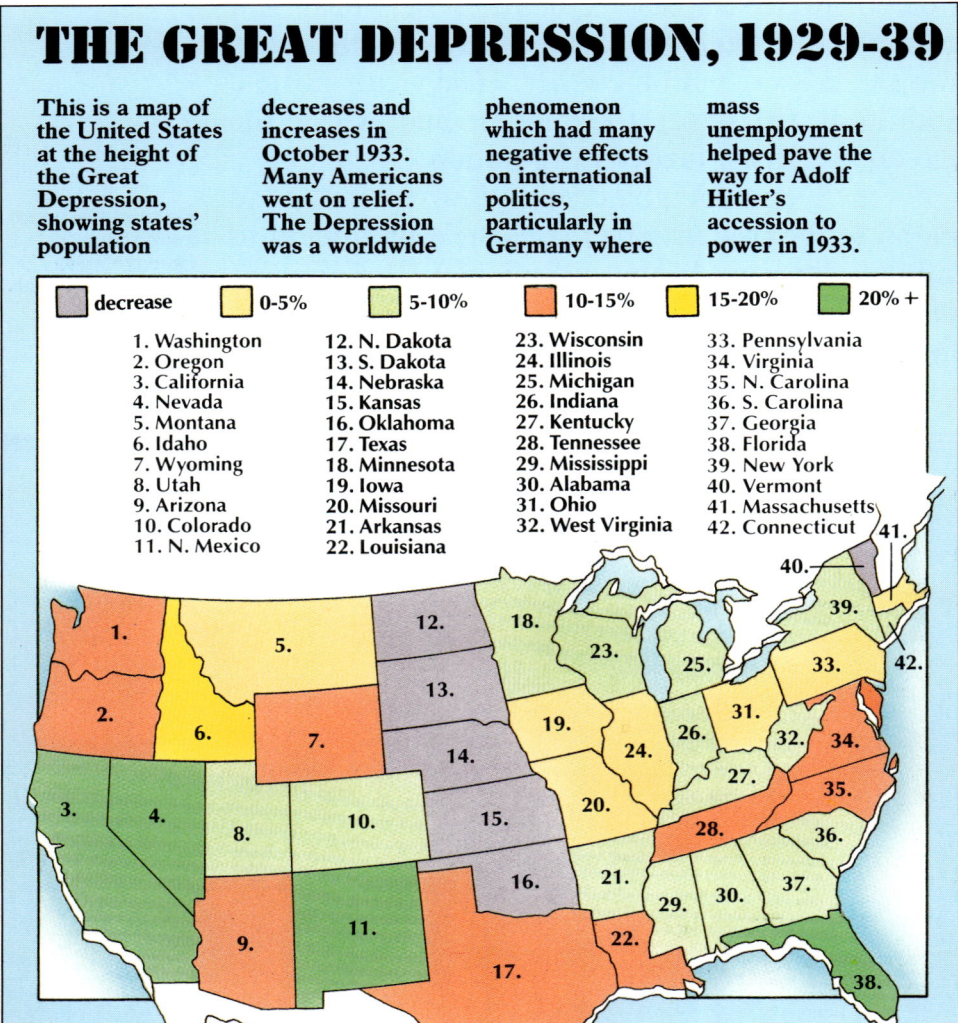

THE GREAT DEPRESSION, 1929-39

This is a map of the United States at the height of the Great Depression, showing states' population decreases and increases in October 1933. Many Americans went on relief. The Depression was a worldwide phenomenon which had many negative effects on international politics, particularly in Germany where mass unemployment helped pave the way for Adolf Hitler's accession to power in 1933.

| decrease | 0-5% | 5-10% | 10-15% | 15-20% | 20% + |

1. Washington
2. Oregon
3. California
4. Nevada
5. Montana
6. Idaho
7. Wyoming
8. Utah
9. Arizona
10. Colorado
11. N. Mexico
12. N. Dakota
13. S. Dakota
14. Nebraska
15. Kansas
16. Oklahoma
17. Texas
18. Minnesota
19. Iowa
20. Missouri
21. Arkansas
22. Louisiana
23. Wisconsin
24. Illinois
25. Michigan
26. Indiana
27. Kentucky
28. Tennessee
29. Mississippi
30. Alabama
31. Ohio
32. West Virginia
33. Pennsylvania
34. Virginia
35. N. Carolina
36. S. Carolina
37. Georgia
38. Florida
39. New York
40. Vermont
41. Massachusetts
42. Connecticut

quietly began to build up support. He assembled around him a group of bright young men who turned his ideas into a coherent programme.

After three cliff-hanging votes at the Democratic Convention in Chicago, Roosevelt secured the two-thirds majority needed for the presidential nomination. In the ensuing campaign Roosevelt demonstrated his new maturity, fighting spirit, and political skill. The details of his programme remained hazy, but he skilfully created the impression that he was a man of action. However, perhaps his greatest electoral asset was the simple fact that he was not Hoover, whose presidency and party were now identified in the public's mind with hard times. Roosevelt's victory was decisive. Only six states voted for Hoover. Congress, too, fell firmly under Democratic control.

Franklin Roosevelt "pressing the flesh", as he greets a farmer on his way to visit the Warm Springs Foundation for polio victims, in Virginia, which he established in 1927. As ever, his disability is artfully concealed from the camera.

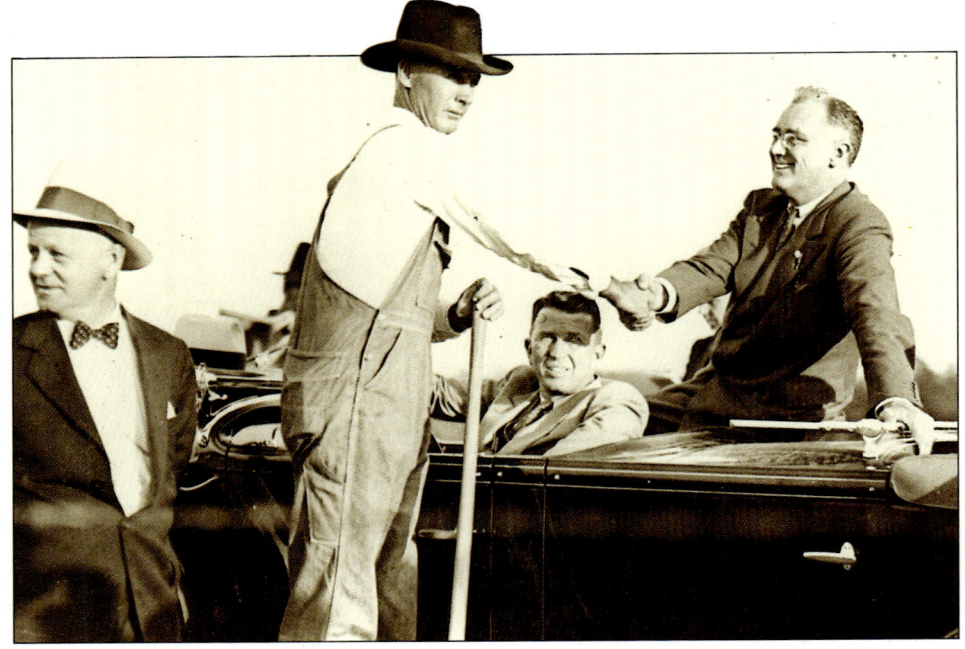

THE NEW DEAL

Roosevelt took centre stage on 4 March 1933, when he swore the oath of office. On the day of his inauguration the banks of New York and Chicago closed their doors. Unrest in the farming regions was approaching open revolt. Industrial production had slumped to 40 per cent of its capacity. The machinery of relief, administered by the states, cities and private charities, had virtually broken down. Roosevelt's response was an electrifying inauguration speech in which he declared: "This nation asks for action, and action now!" In what was to become the rallying cry of his peacetime presidency, he promised "a new deal for the American people".

Roosevelt takes the oath of office in March 1933 in a climate of threatening economic collapse and growing social chaos.

In 1932 Roosevelt had suggested that "the country needs and, unless I mistake its temper, the country demands, bold, persistent experimentation." Congress was called into a special session lasting the now legendary "hundred days". It enacted 13 major measures, covering almost every aspect of the nation's economic life. Among them was an Emergency Banking Act, a Federal Relief Emergency Act, a National Industrial Recovery Act, an Agricultural Adjustment Act, an Emergency Farm Mortgage Act, and, to cheer the nation up, the end of Prohibition (the ban on the manufacture and sale of alcohol, in force since 1920). As Roosevelt put it, in the casual way which was to become the hallmark of his presidency, "I think this would be a good time for beer."

Numerous executive agencies were established to carry out the programme of national recovery,

The Watts Bar dam under construction on the Tennessee River, part of a massive programme of public works undertaken by the Tennessee Valley Authority as part of the New Deal.

including the Civilian Conservation Corps, which eventually took 2.5 million jobless men and boys off the streets to undertake massive afforestation projects. The Tennessee Valley Authority was also set up, which reclaimed a huge area of derelict rural America while generating cheap electrical power from federally-built and -operated dams.

Hand-in-hand with these measures came the re-organisation of the banking system and the establishment of the Securities and Exchange Commission to clean up and supervise the stock market. The emergence of an American welfare state was marked by the establishment of a federally-sponsored unemployment insurance pro- gramme and an old age pension. The unionisation of industry was encouraged, and sweatshops and child labour were curbed by the stipulation of minimum hours and working conditions.

FDR signs the Social Security Bill on 14 August 1935. Standing immediately behind him is his Secretary of Labor, Frances Perkins, a key figure in the welfare reforms created under the New Deal.

The New Deal did not provide an instant cure for the United States' economic ills, but its impact was greatest among the labour force and ethnic groups, not least the black population. These groups formed the basis of a new political coalition which carried Roosevelt through to an overwhelming victory in the presidential election of 1936. The "Roosevelt coalition" lasted not only throughout his lifetime but for many years after.

The New Deal, however, ran into problems. In the spring of 1937, production levels had returned to those of 1929, but in the autumn the economy was overtaken by another slump. In large part the slump had been brought on by Roosevelt's insistence on balancing the budget. In 1938 unemployment climbed back to 19 per cent. The steam was running out of the New Deal. In the spring of 1938 Roosevelt enacted a burst of new legislation and the introduction of an emergency $3,750 million spending programme. This measure lessened the crisis.

The successes and failures of the New Deal are closely linked with the strengths and weaknesses of Roosevelt's style of governing. On a directly personal level he accustomed the American people to turn to the White House for solutions to their political problems. He was always news, his confident grin splashed across the front pages of the newspapers, whose reporters he entertained at informal twice-weekly press conferences. His self-belief communicated itself to ordinary Americans through his regular "fireside" radio broadcasts. The American people not only regained some of their former prosperity under the New Deal, but also began to rebuild their self-respect.

However, much of what Roosevelt achieved might have been forced on any president – even a conservative like Herbert Hoover – simply because of the gravity of the Depression. In this sense Roosevelt was an accelerator of social reforms rather than an innovator. Unquestionably, by his actions during these difficult times Roosevelt preserved a democratic "middle way" in America at a time when much of Europe was being swept by totalitarianism.

The way to war

On the day Roosevelt took office in 1933, Japanese troops marched into the provincial capital of Jehol in China. On the next day Adolf Hitler was confirmed as chancellor of Germany. Hitler was

Adolf Hitler climbs the steps to the podium at a Nazi Party rally. By the mid-1930s Hitler had embarked on a course that would ultimately lead to World War II.

convinced that his destiny was to reverse Germany's World War I defeat and restore the nation as a world power.

In the mid-1930s Hitler presided over an impressive German recovery from the ravages of the Depression, achieved by a policy of not balancing the country's budget – a policy from which Roosevelt had shrunk. Hitler was not worried about a budget deficit, and the resulting economic recovery financed German rearmament. Skillful propaganda concealed the underlying weakness of Germany's rapidly expanding armed forces, and their strength was consistently overestimated abroad. War, or the threat of it, was the dynamic of Hitler's foreign policy in the 1930s.

In March 1936 Hitler re-occupied the demilitarised Rhineland, against the advice of his senior commanders. Britain and France failed to react and Hitler embarked on an increasingly aggressive foreign policy. In March 1938 he annexed Austria. This opened his way to Czechoslovakia, whose Sudetenland on its western border contained a large German minority. In September 1938 Hitler outmanoeuvred the British Prime Minister Neville Chamberlain at the Munich conference to gain control of the Sudetenland over the heads of the Czechs. In March 1939 Hitler swallowed up the rest of Czechoslovakia.

He then turned his attention north to the Baltic, the free port of Danzig, and the "Polish Corridor" which separated Germany from East Prussia. His demands that the Poles restore Danzig to Germany were turned down by the Polish government. On 23 March, German troops occupied Memel, on the border of East Prussia and Lithuania. Poland warned Hitler that any similar attempt to seize Danzig would mean war. A week later Britain and France declared that they would stand by Poland. The democracies were now bracing themselves for what seemed the inevitable outbreak of war.

Roosevelt had been quick to grasp the threat posed by the ruthless expansionist policies of Germany, Japan and Italy, whose dictator, Benito Mussolini, had invaded Ethiopia (Abyssinia) in 1935. But deep-seated isolationist and pacifist opinion at home left him with little room to manoeuvre, while the demands of the New Deal forced him to focus on domestic issues.

In the 1930s, Roosevelt's foreign policy proceeded by fits and starts. When he attempted to use his influence in European affairs, Congress would not allow it. In 1935 it passed the first of a series of neutrality measures which prohibited private loans or credits to nations at war ("belligerent nations"), embargoed shipments of arms and munitions to belligerents, and stipulated "cash and carry" for any other articles. In the future, belligerents who wanted to buy non-military goods would have to pay cash on the nail for them and transport them in their own ships or those of a country other than the United States.

Roosevelt was powerless to intervene when Italy invaded Ethiopia and Germany marched into the Rhineland, and by the summer of 1936 Roosevelt appeared to have succumbed to the prevailing pacifist mood in America. In a speech delivered at Chautauqua he stated: "We shun political commitments which might entangle us in foreign wars." Recalling his battlefield tour of 1918, he told his audience, "I have seen war. . . . I have seen the dead in the mud. . . . I have seen cities destroyed. . . . I have seen children starving. . . . I hate war."

In the election year of 1936 he pursued a "hands-off" policy when General Francisco Franco rebelled against the government of Spain. Franco received heavy military assistance from Germany and Italy. The neutrality measures did not apply to civil wars, and Roosevelt could have recognised the right of the legitimate government of Spain to buy arms from the United States.

By 1937 Roosevelt was deeply troubled not only by events in Europe but by continued Japanese aggression in the Far East. In July Japan went to war with China. By the end of the year Shanghai had been subjected to a ferocious aerial bombardment and Nanking endured six weeks of rape and pillage that shocked the world.

While still committed to peace, Roosevelt began to look for a way to bring international pressure to bear on Germany, Italy and Japan. In October 1937, in a speech delivered in Chicago, where isolationist sentiment was at its strongest, Roosevelt warned that an "epidemic of world lawlessness" was spreading. He said, "When an epidemic of physical disease starts to spread, the community approves and joins in a quarantine of the patients in order to protect the health of the community against the spread of the disease."

The "quarantine speech" was interpreted as a fresh departure in American foreign policy: the abandonment of isolationism and the issuing of a

direct warning to Japan. But Roosevelt's intentions were altogether more ambiguous. In truth he had no policy. When an aide asked him what precisely he meant by the quarantine speech, he replied, "I can't give you any clue to it. You will have to invent one." When on 12 December 1937 Japanese warplanes sank an American gunship, the USS *Panay*, while it was patrolling the Yangtze River, Roosevelt was quick to accept Japan's apologies and an indemnity.

As war in Europe approached, the United States remained determinedly neutral. Roosevelt's desire to aid the democracies was severely limited by the Neutrality Acts. Nevertheless, the United States government gave the British and French the

The worries of office show clearly on FDR's face as he drives to the White House with his Secretary of State, Cordell Hull, on 29 August 1939, three days before Germany invaded Poland.

go-ahead to place large orders for aircraft with American manufacturers – the first step in a massive industrial expansion. But Roosevelt failed to drag Congress along with him; in mid-summer Congress refused to modify the Neutrality Acts.

In September 1939 Poland was overrun by German and Soviet troops in a campaign lasting five weeks. In the United States there was a fierce debate about what should be done. The rapid collapse of Poland had come as a shock. Roosevelt responded by calling Congress into special session and asking it to amend the Neutrality Acts so that arms could be supplied to the French and British. A six-week debate produced an amendment which allowed belligerents to buy war materials on a "cash and carry" basis. There seemed no reason why the United States should not profit from the troubles of the British and the French.

On 10 May 1940 Hitler launched a devastating offensive in western Europe. The Dutch surrendered on 15 May after an aerial bombardment of Rotterdam. Belgium capitulated on 27 May, as the British Expeditionary Force (BEF) was beginning its evacuation from Dunkirk. By the small hours of 4 June, 338,000 British and French troops had been taken to safety, but the BEF had left all of its heavy equipment behind. On 14 June German troops entered Paris, and eight days later the French signed a humiliating armistice. The British prepared to face a German invasion.

On 22 June 1940 Congress passed a National Defense Tax Bill and a month later voted $37 billion – more than the entire American cost of World War I – to produce a "two-ocean" navy and a massively expanded army and air force.

Roosevelt was now nominated for an unprecedented third term. Isolationists charged that he was dragging the nation into war. However, support for Britain, fighting for its life against the German Air Force, was growing. In July 1940 the British prime minister, Winston Churchill, appealed to Roosevelt for 50 old destroyers. In an act which was technically illegal, Roosevelt provided the destroyers, but at the price of 99-year leases on a number of naval and air bases in the British West Indies and Bermuda.

Military preparation was now at the top of the political agenda in the United States. In September 1940, as the Battle of Britain reached its climax, Congress passed the Selective Training and Service Act to draft men between the ages of 21 and 36. At first the army was short of everything except bodies, but slowly the production gears began to turn. American industrial and military might would be the key element in the war.

Roosevelt was re-elected in November. When Congress met in January 1941 he appealed to it to support the nations that were fighting in defence of what he called the Four Freedoms: freedom of speech, freedom of religion, freedom from want, freedom from fear. These were fine resounding words, but what the British needed, above all else, was an arms supply on easier terms than those of "cash and carry", which they could no longer afford to pay.

Roosevelt's answer was the Lend-Lease Act, passed by Congress in March 1941. The Act allowed the British to borrow war supplies from

Firmly gripping the arm of his son, the only way he could maintain his balance, FDR greets Winston Churchill at Placentia Bay, Newfoundland, in August 1941. Churchill was careful to play on American popular feeling, aware that American help in the war was of the utmost importance to Britain's survival.

the United States against the promise of later repayment. By the end of the month Congress had voted Lend-Lease a colossal $7 billion, the first installment in a programme to arm and feed the Allies which would total over $50 billion.

In taking "all steps short of war" to sustain the British, Roosevelt was edging the United States towards war. At the end of March, Axis ships in US ports were seized. In May, 50 oil tankers were transferred to Britain. On 28 May, following the torpedoing of the American freighter *Robin Moor* by a U-boat, Roosevelt declared a state of un-limited national emergency. Axis credit in the United States was frozen and Axis consulates closed in June. In July, US Marines replaced British troops in Iceland, which the British had occupied after the fall of Denmark in 1940.

On 9 August, at Placentia Bay in Newfoundland, Roosevelt and Churchill met to discuss their war aims. They agreed that the destruction of Nazi Germany was the foremost priority and issued the Atlantic Charter, which embodied Roosevelt's Four Freedoms, and provided the seed from which the United Nations grew. However, it was typical of the Roosevelt style that the strategy agreed upon at Placentia Bay – that of joint American and British military and political action – could not take effect until the United States was at war with Germany.

In the Atlantic the US Navy was already engaged in a war of sorts. Since the beginning of the war Roosevelt had extended American protection to Britain-bound convoys in the Atlantic. At first he had defined a neutrality zone which denied U-boats access to American waters, and from April 1941 he extended the zone to the mid-ocean boundary and allowed US warships to act as convoy escorts.

On 31 October 1941 a U-boat sank the old four-stack destroyer USS *Reuben James*, killing 115 American sailors. Within two weeks Congress had moved to arm merchantmen and permit them to sail directly into war zones. But Roosevelt still did not act. A bigger shock was needed to bring the United States into war. Hitler seemed unlikely to oblige. His attention was fixed on the Eastern Front as his armies drove ever deeper into the Soviet Union. Roosevelt told his Secretary of the Treasury, Henry Morgenthau, "I am waiting to be pushed into the situation." When the shove came it was from a different direction, the Far East.

AMERICA GOES TO WAR

The United States had stood aside as the Japanese Army secured the entire coast of China and large tracts of its interior. It was not until September 1940 that Roosevelt acted to halt the Japanese advance, which now extended to French Indochina. He chose an economic weapon, imposing an embargo on rubber which was followed in July 1941 by the freezing of all Japanese assets in the United States and the announcement of an oil embargo against all aggressors, a category which included Japan.

Wearing a black armband, a grim-faced Roosevelt signs America's declaration of war against Japan following the attack on Pearl Harbor.

At a stroke the Japanese were deprived of 90 per cent of their oil supplies and 75 per cent of their foreign trade. If they could not secure new supplies of raw materials, they would be forced to relinquish the Chinese territory gained in years of hard fighting and suffer a humiliating loss of face. In the words of Admiral Osami Nagano, Chief of the Japanese General Staff, Japan was like "a fish in a pond from which the water is gradually being drained away".

Alternative sources of raw materials were relatively near at hand, in Borneo, Java, Sumatra, Malaya and Burma. The only way to obtain them was to undertake the rapid military conquest of a vast area of the Far East. Inevitably, this would bring Japan into conflict with the United States. In November 1941 US-Japanese talks began in Washington DC with the goal of averting hostilities. The Americans were well aware of Japanese intentions; they had been decoding and reading Japanese messages for months. But they remained ignorant of the precise Japanese plans. Drawn up by Admiral Isoruku Yamamoto, Commander-in-Chief of the Japanese Combined Fleet, they had been approved by Admiral Nagano on 3 November. The initial offensive would be directed against Pearl Harbor, and then the Philippines and Malaya, followed by the Dutch East Indies. Pearl Harbor, on the Hawaiian island of Oahu, the operational and training base of the US Pacific Fleet and 5,471 km (3,400 miles) distant from Japan, was to be attacked by a striking force of aircraft carriers.

At 7.55 am on 7 December the Japanese struck

at Pearl Harbor, achieving complete surprise. Shortly before 1.00 pm on the 8th, Roosevelt asked Congress to declare war on Japan. He began, "Yesterday, December 7, 1941, a day that will live in infamy, the United States of America was suddenly and deliberately attacked by naval and air forces of the Empire of Japan." The speech was greeted with thunderous applause. He had spoken for all Americans. Britain had declared war on Japan earlier the same day. Three days later Germany and Italy – honouring treaty obligations with Japan – declared war on the United States. Churchill instantly recognised that this was a turning point. With the United States' vast military potential now fully engaged, his first thought was, "we have won the war." Later he wrote that he went to bed that night and slept "the sleep of the saved and the thankful".

In the United States there was an overwhelming feeling of relief now that the waiting was over and their country was engaged in the war. The pressures exerted by the isolationists were lifted and the nation entered the war in a mood of optimism untainted by the setbacks which had afflicted its ally Britain, and the humiliating defeat which had knocked France out of the war. There was, however, an immediate and harsh reaction against the American-Japanese community, the majority of whom lived in California. Many thousands were interned, often in grim conditions, as a measure of national security. Their fate reflected the anti-Japanese hysteria which ran through the United States after Pearl Harbor, and remains a blot on the human rights record of the United States.

DAY OF INFAMY

At 6.30 am on 7 December 1941, 214 bombers and fighters took off from six Japanese aircraft carriers lying 443 km north of the US naval base at Pearl Harbor on the Hawaiian island of Oahu. They were the first wave in a surprise attack launched without a formal declaration of war. The 94 US warships and auxiliaries anchored in Pearl Harbor were sitting targets. The first wave of Japanese warplanes burst through the clouds over Pearl Harbor at 7.55 am and were followed by a second wave an hour later. They succeeded in sinking or disabling all eight battleships and destroyed over 300 aircraft on the ground. One vital factor mitigated the Japanese victory: the US Pacific Fleet's aircraft carriers were on a training cruise and escaped attack.

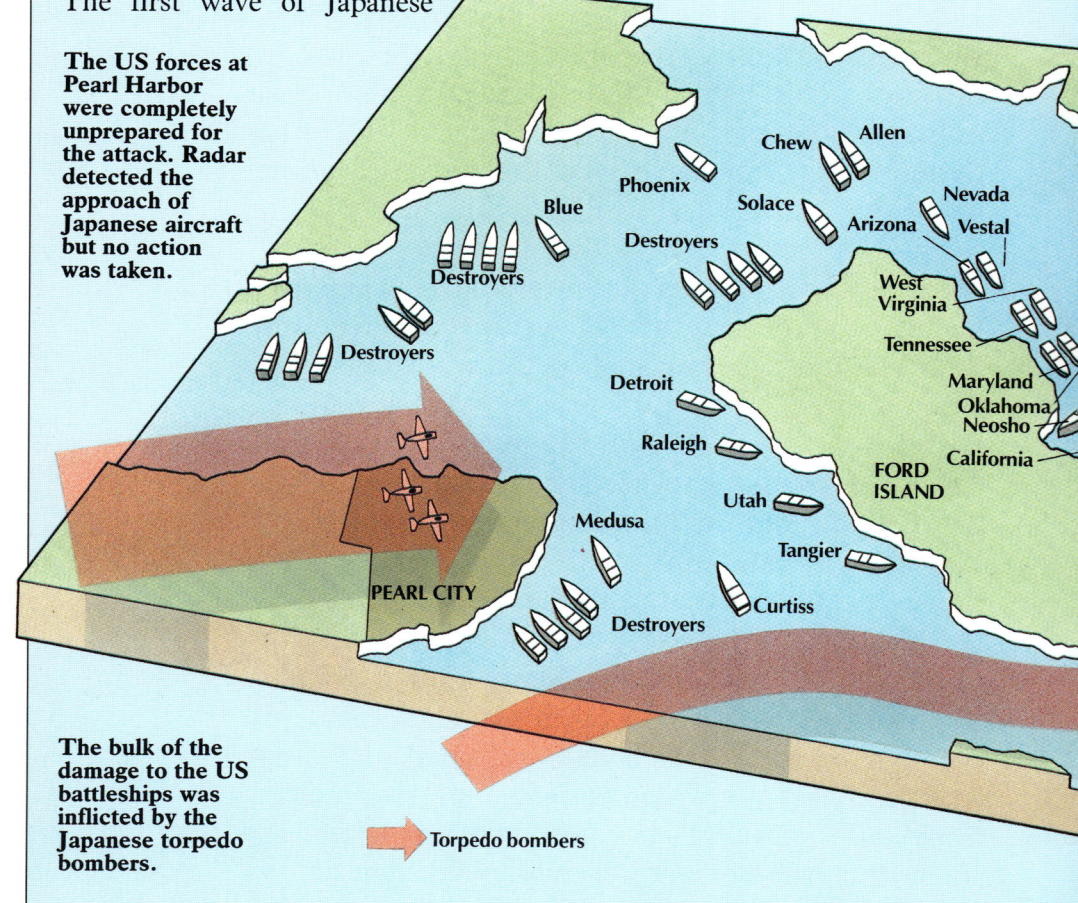

The US forces at Pearl Harbor were completely unprepared for the attack. Radar detected the approach of Japanese aircraft but no action was taken.

The bulk of the damage to the US battleships was inflicted by the Japanese torpedo bombers.

Torpedo bombers

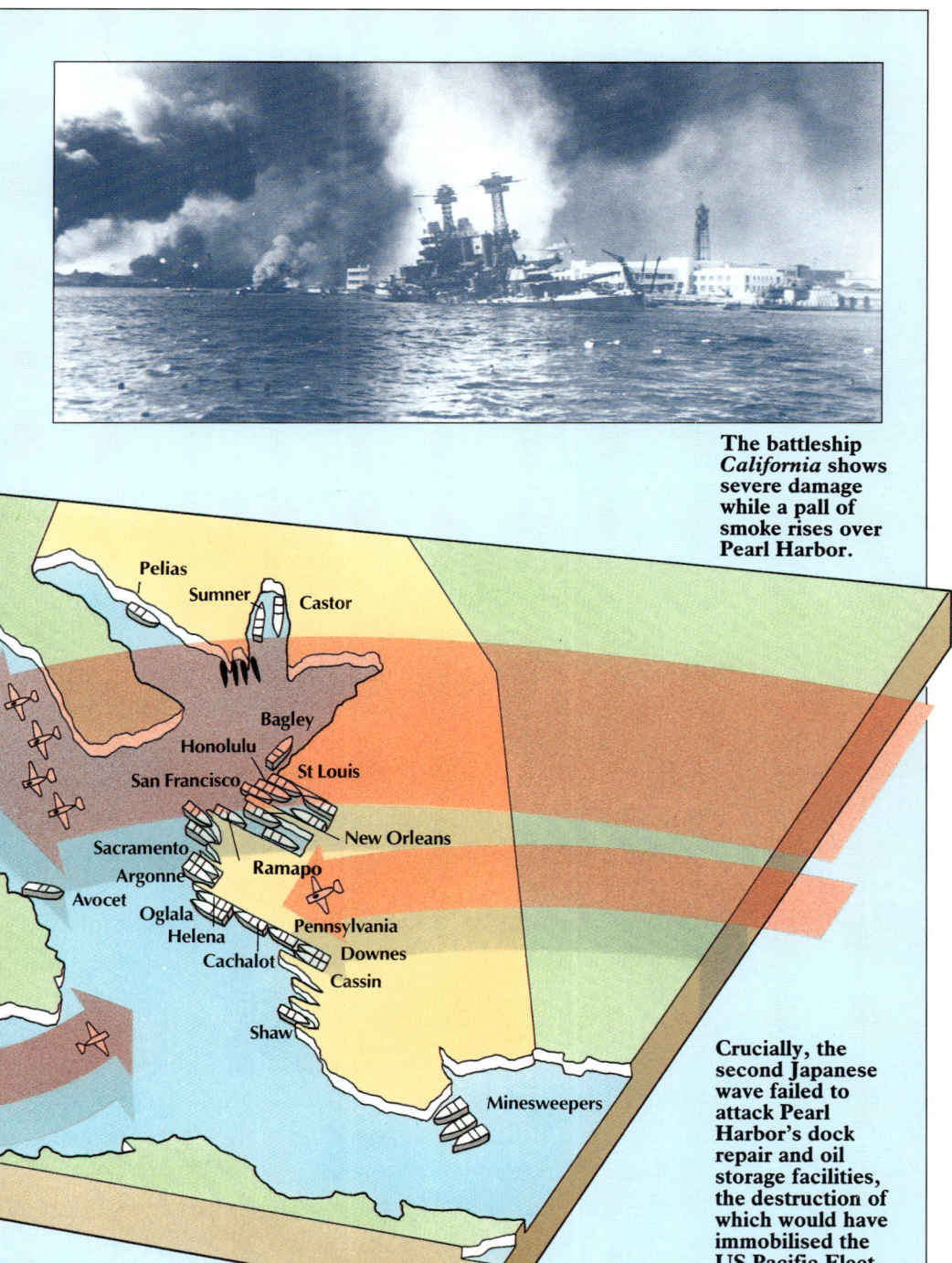

The battleship *California* shows severe damage while a pall of smoke rises over Pearl Harbor.

Pelias
Sumner
Castor
Bagley
Honolulu
San Francisco
St Louis
New Orleans
Sacramento
Argonne
Ramapo
Avocet
Oglala
Pennsylvania
Helena
Downes
Cachalot
Cassin
Shaw
Minesweepers

Crucially, the second Japanese wave failed to attack Pearl Harbor's dock repair and oil storage facilities, the destruction of which would have immobilised the US Pacific Fleet.

On 22 December, Churchill, Roosevelt and their respective staffs met in Washington DC for a conference codenamed "Arcadia". In formulating a general policy for fighting the war they were guided by the ABC-1 plan, which the two staffs had drawn up a year before, when the United States was still on the sidelines of the war. In spite of intense pressure from his admirals that the Japanese threat in the Pacific must take the top priority, Roosevelt confirmed the "Germany First" policy which had been agreed at Placentia Bay. To achieve this, both sides agreed that the continent of Europe would have to be invaded and that Britain would be the springboard for this operation. Furthermore, at all costs the Soviet Union was to be kept in the war, and this could only be achieved by extending to the Soviet leader, Josef Stalin, the terms of Lend-Lease. A more thorny problem was presented by the strategic priorities in the Mediterranean. The British were eager to clear the coast of North Africa before setting foot on continental Europe. The Americans considered this an unwelcome diversion from the principal objective of invading Europe at the earliest opportunity. Eventually a compromise was reached; plans were to be drawn up for a joint invasion of North Africa, which would not be feasible until May 1942 at the earliest.

It escaped no one's attention that the Arcadia conference took place against a background of full-blown military disaster in the Far East. Neither the Americans nor the colonial powers in the Pacific (Britain and the Netherlands) were in any way prepared to stem the tide of Japanese conquest. For six months the Japanese were able to carve out a huge Pacific empire that put even Hitler's victories to shame. By May 1942 the islands of Guam and Wake, the Philippines, French Indochina, Burma, Thailand, Malaya, Singapore, Hong Kong, the Dutch East Indies, three-quarters of New Guinea and Papua, the

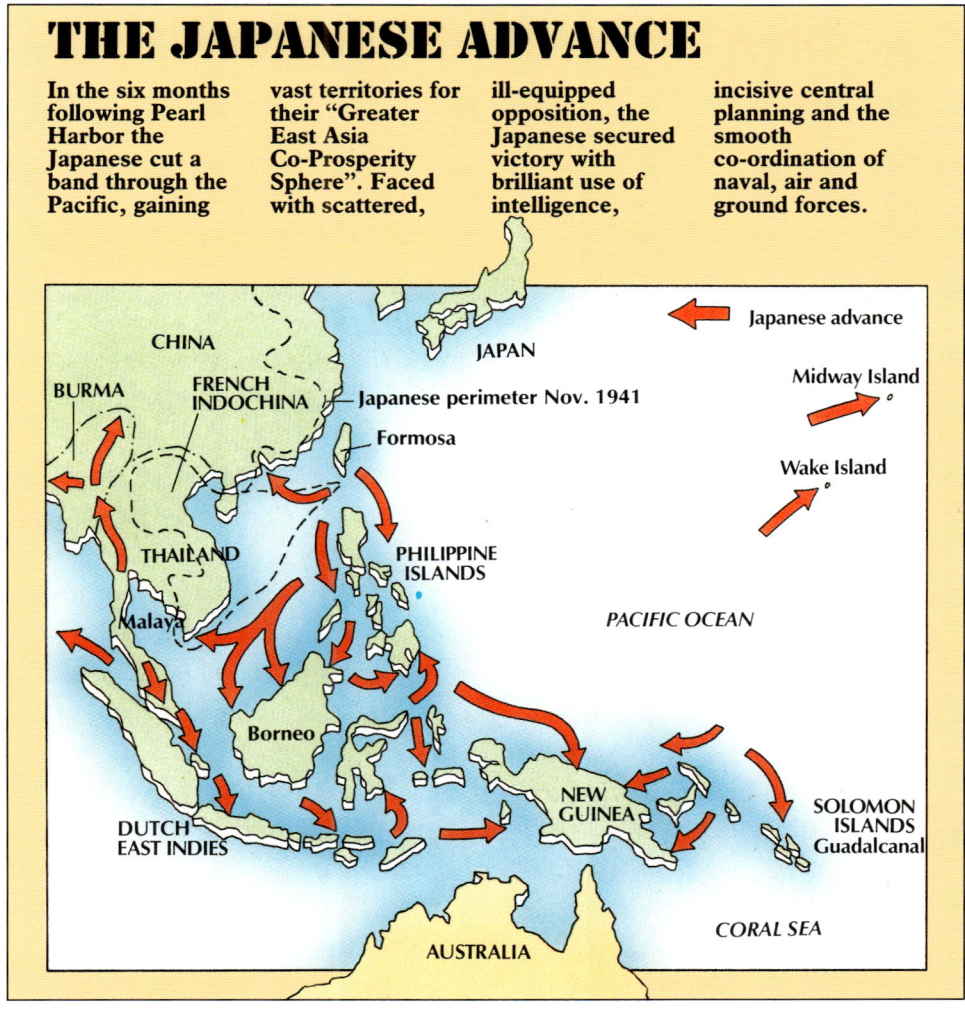

THE JAPANESE ADVANCE

In the six months following Pearl Harbor the Japanese cut a band through the Pacific, gaining vast territories for their "Greater East Asia Co-Prosperity Sphere". Faced with scattered, ill-equipped opposition, the Japanese secured victory with brilliant use of intelligence, incisive central planning and the smooth co-ordination of naval, air and ground forces.

The US aircraft carrier *Yorktown* receives a direct hit at the Battle of Midway on 4 June 1942. Although the *Yorktown* was sunk, the US Pacific Fleet, commanded by Admiral Nimitz, won a great victory, sinking three Japanese carriers. Fought at long-range with carrier-borne aircraft, Midway was the first naval battle in which the opposing capital ships never saw each other.

Bismarck Archipelago and a substantial part of the Gilbert and Solomon Islands were in their hands. To the north, they threatened the Aleutian chain and the approaches to Alaska; in the west they were close to the borders of India; to the south they menaced Australia.

To secure this vast perimeter, the Japanese sought to lure into battle and destroy the US Pacific Fleet. In two crucial naval encounters, Coral Sea (4-8 May 1942) and Midway (4 June), the Japanese were first halted and then decisively defeated by Admiral Chester W Nimitz's aircraft carriers, the warships which were to dominate operations in the Pacific War. The all-conquering Japanese were now forced to defend a vast ocean empire which might be attacked at any point by the gathering might of the American war machine.

The point the Americans chose was the Solomons chain. On 7 August 1942 US Marines stormed ashore at Guadalcanal, the first move in an epic battle which marked the beginning of the Allied reconquest of the Pacific.

Guadalcanal was finally secured on 9 February 1943. Six days earlier, in Germany, Adolf Hitler had proclaimed four days of national mourning following the annihilation of Field Marshal Friedrich Paulus' Sixth Army at Stalingrad. In North Africa the "Torch" landings in Morocco and Algeria, and the British victory at El Alamein (November 1942) had been followed by a long, hard fight for Tunisia which was brought to a successful conclusion in May. In the Atlantic the battle against the U-boats was swinging the Allies' way. On all fronts the strategic initiative had passed from the Axis to the Allies.

Allied success made it all the more important to secure agreement on a common strategy. At the Casablanca conference (13-24 January 1943) in Morocco, Roosevelt and Churchill reached a number of important decisions: to invade Sicily; to mount a joint bomber offensive against Germany; to accelerate the build-up of US troops in the United Kingdom in readiness for an invasion of Europe; and to demand the "unconditional surrender" of Germany, Italy and Japan.

The insistence on "unconditional surrender" had stemmed largely from Roosevelt. It underlined the differences between Roosevelt's role and style as commander-in-chief and those of the other warlords, Churchill, Hitler and Stalin. Churchill revelled in the whole business of warmaking,

THE B-17 "FLYING FORTRESS"

This Boeing long-range bomber was the symbol of the US Army Air Force's belief that victory could be secured by high-level precision daylight bombing of the enemy's key industrial targets.

This theory was tested almost to the point of disaster in the skies over Germany in 1943 when B-17s and B-24 Liberators suffered heavy losses at the hands of the *Luftwaffe* (German Air Force). The bombers, flying in mass formation, could not fight their way to and from their targets without suffering unacceptable losses. The situation was improved in December 1943 with the introduction of the powerful P-51 Mustang escort fighter.

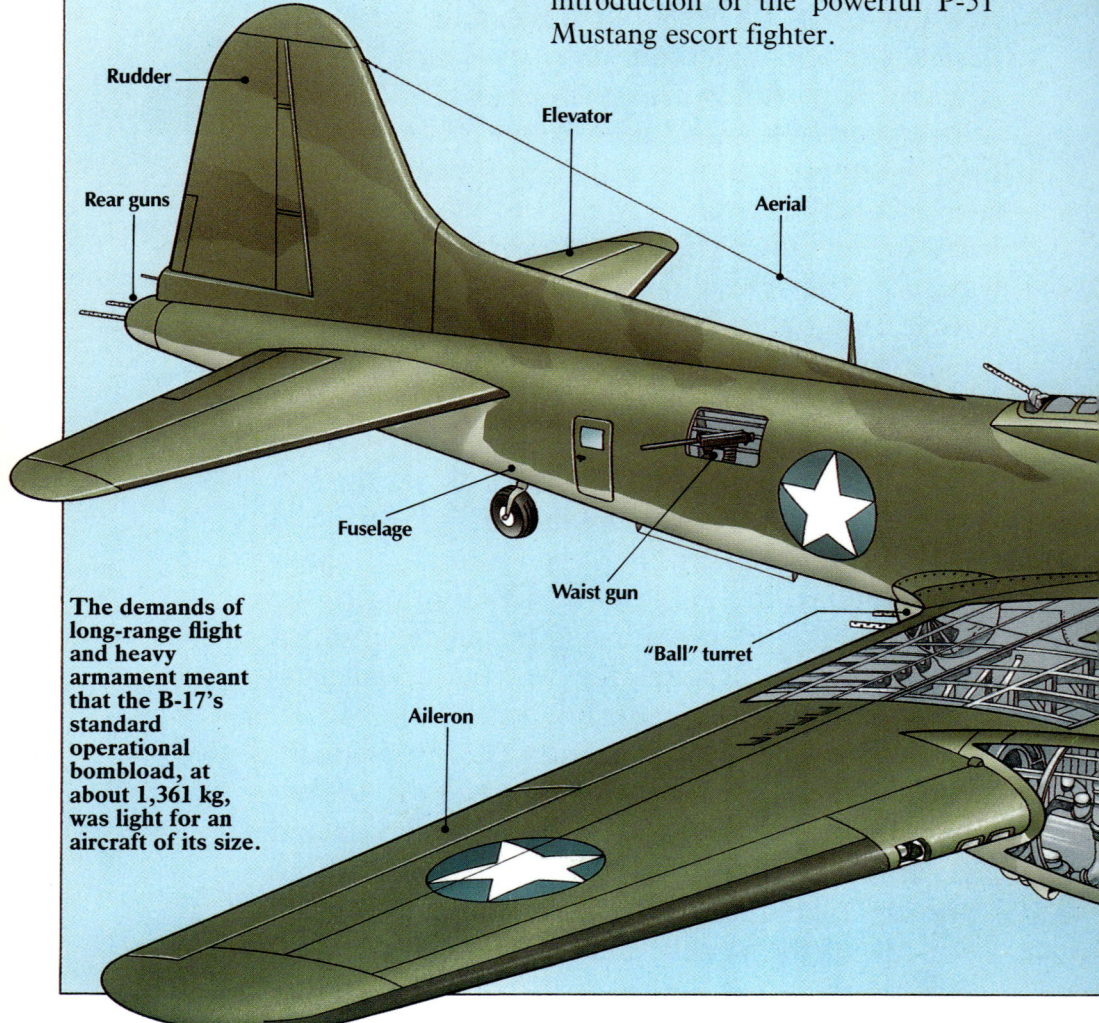

Rudder

Elevator

Aerial

Rear guns

Fuselage

Waist gun

"Ball" turret

Aileron

The demands of long-range flight and heavy armament meant that the B-17's standard operational bombload, at about 1,361 kg, was light for an aircraft of its size.

Cockpit

Gun turret

Bomb bay

B-17Gs of the US
8th Army Air
Force, based in
England, unload
their bombs over
Germany.

Nose gun

Propeller

Engine

By August 1944,
4,600 B-17s were
at the war fronts
in 33 bombing
groups. The
B-17s remained

the backbone of
the US Army Air
Force's strategic
bombing effort in
Europe until the
end of the war.

General Giraud (left), Roosevelt, General de Gaulle, commander-in-chief of the Free French Army, and Winston Churchill at the Casablanca conference in January 1943. Their uneasy-looking mood reflects the poor relations between Roosevelt and de Gaulle.

spending his days (and nights) in constant contact with his military advisers. The potentially dangerous effects of Churchill's persistent meddling and wilder flights of fancy were mitigated by Field Marshal Sir Alan Brooke, Chief of the Imperial General Staff. No such restraints applied to Hitler, whose paranoid suspicion of his generals and morbid preoccupation with every detail of military operations was to prove disastrous. Stalin followed a similar nocturnal, secretive routine, fighting the war through capable subordinates like Marshal Georgi Zhukov.

In contrast, Roosevelt remained aloof from the business of running the war. After Pearl Harbor he scarcely altered the pattern of his life: work in the White House seldom began before 10.00 am, and he took few telephone calls at night. According to James MacGregor Burns: "He saw the Congressional Big Four – the vice president, the Speaker of the House and the majority leader of each chamber – on Monday or Tuesday; met with the press on Tuesday afternoons and Friday mornings; and presided over a Cabinet meeting on Friday afternoons. There seemed to be no pattern at all in the way Roosevelt did his work. Sometimes he hurried through appointments on crucial matters and dawdled during lesser ones. He ignored most letters altogether. . . . He took many phone calls, refused others, saw inconsequential and dull people, and ignored others of apparently greater political or intellectual weight – all according to some mystifying structure of priorities known to no one, perhaps not even himself."

Restricted by his disability, Roosevelt travelled sparingly during the war: to conferences at Casablanca in 1943, Quebec twice (August 1943 and September 1944), Teheran (November 1943) and

FDR in a genial mood as Churchill's daughter Sarah is introduced to Josef Stalin at Teheran in 1943.

Cairo (November/December 1943), and Yalta in the Soviet Crimea (February 1945). Roosevelt saw none of the consequences of war – ruined towns, columns of prisoners, civilian refugees – that he had witnessed in 1918. His was a peacetime routine while leading a nation that was not only physically untouched by war but was also growing immeasurably rich through waging it.

In 1939 the US economy was still in a depressed state. Mobilisation for war, which began before the attack on Pearl Harbor, produced an economic surge which released the almost boundless power of American industry. In 1939 the United States was a negligible producer of military equipment; by 1944 it was producing 40 per cent of the world's armaments. In 1940 it had built only 346 tanks; four years later 17,500 tanks rolled off American production lines. The figures for aircraft production in 1940 of 2,141 aircraft leapt to 96,318 in 1944. The Red Army's offensives on the Eastern Front were supported by hundreds of thousands of rugged Ford trucks. The war in the Pacific could be sustained only by a nation rich in manpower and material resources. One Ford plant alone employed 42,000 people. During the course of the war the United States provided civil and military aid to its allies sufficient for it to equip 2,000 infantry divisions. In short, the sheer size and efficiency of the American economy spelled doom for Germany and Japan.

The war also brought important social consequences, a kind of second New Deal. Women found opportunities in aircraft plants and shipyards, and the net effect was to bring a permanent increase in the proportion of women in the labour force. The war brought unparalleled prosperity to millions of Americans. Between 1940 and 1945 the farmers' net cash income more than quadrupled; the weekly wages of industrial workers rose by 70 per cent.

It was this productive capacity which underpinned the invasion of Europe when it came in June

D-DAY LANDINGS, 6 JUNE 1944

The invasion of Normandy (Operation Overlord) was launched on 6 June 1944 (D-Day). After a month-long air offensive and an Allied deception plan which convinced Hitler that the main attack would come in the Pas de Calais, the largest amphibious operation in history got under way. By midnight on 6 June, 57,500 US and 75,000 British and Canadian troops had been landed. It took six weeks of hard fighting before the Allied forces were able to break out into Normandy and form a pincer movement which trapped over 50,000 German soldiers. Paris was liberated on 25 August 1944.

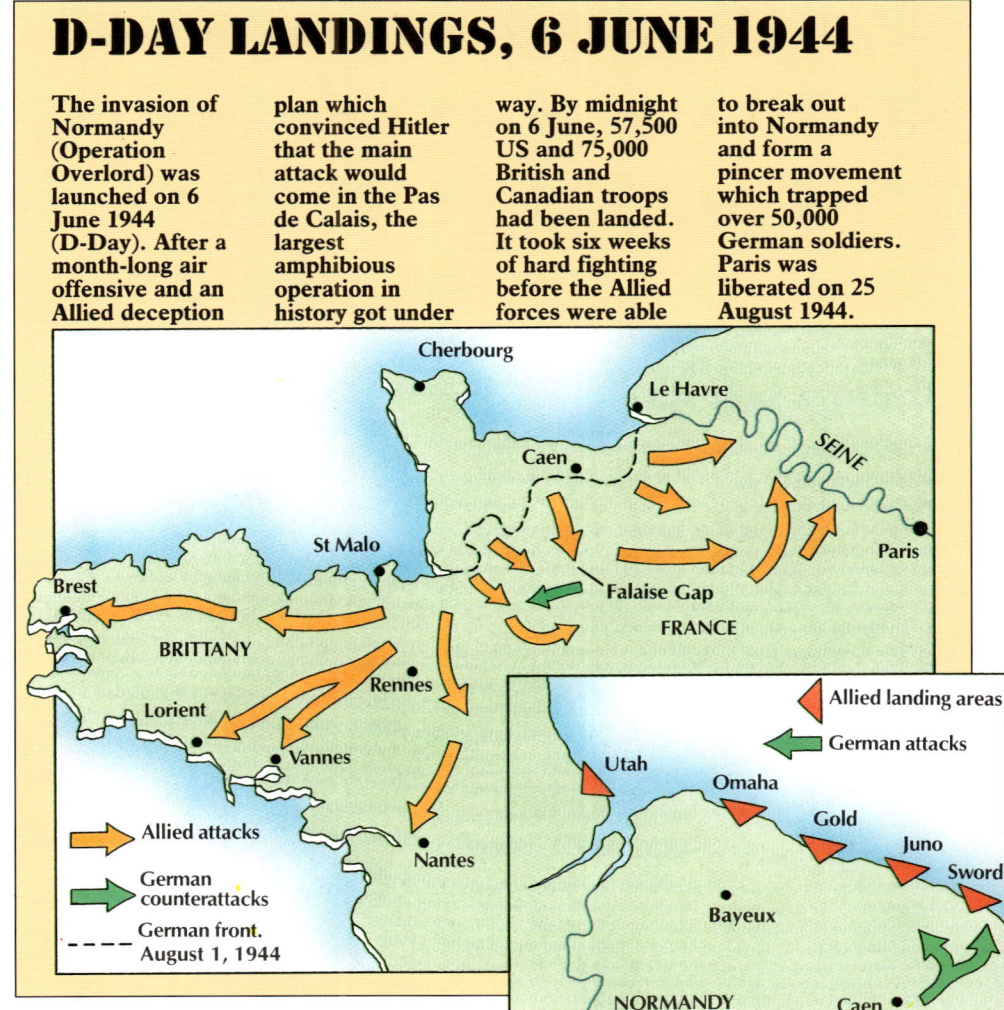

Churchill, Roosevelt and Stalin at Yalta in February 1945. FDR's gaunt features and painfully wasted limbs were shocking proof that his life was fast ebbing away.

1944. In the words of Allan Nevins, the Allied armies "lurched forward like a vast armed workshop; a congeries of factories on wheels with a bristling screen of troops and a cover of aircraft".

Road to victory

Since the beginning of 1944, Roosevelt's health had been deteriorating. His opponents had tried to exploit this during the presidential campaign of 1944, when he ran for a fourth term against Governor Thomas E Dewey, but a last burst of vigour by Roosevelt temporarily laid the rumours of his ill health to rest.

However, by the time he arrived to meet Churchill and Stalin at Yalta in February 1945, Roosevelt was a very sick man. He was painfully thin and gaunt. Churchill's doctor took one look at the president and predicted he would live only a few months more. In Europe the war, too, was nearing its end. The Red Army was only 81 km from Berlin. In the Far East the advance had been slower. The Pacific drive had been leapfrogging toward Japan in a strategy dubbed "island hopping". One by one the island stepping stones

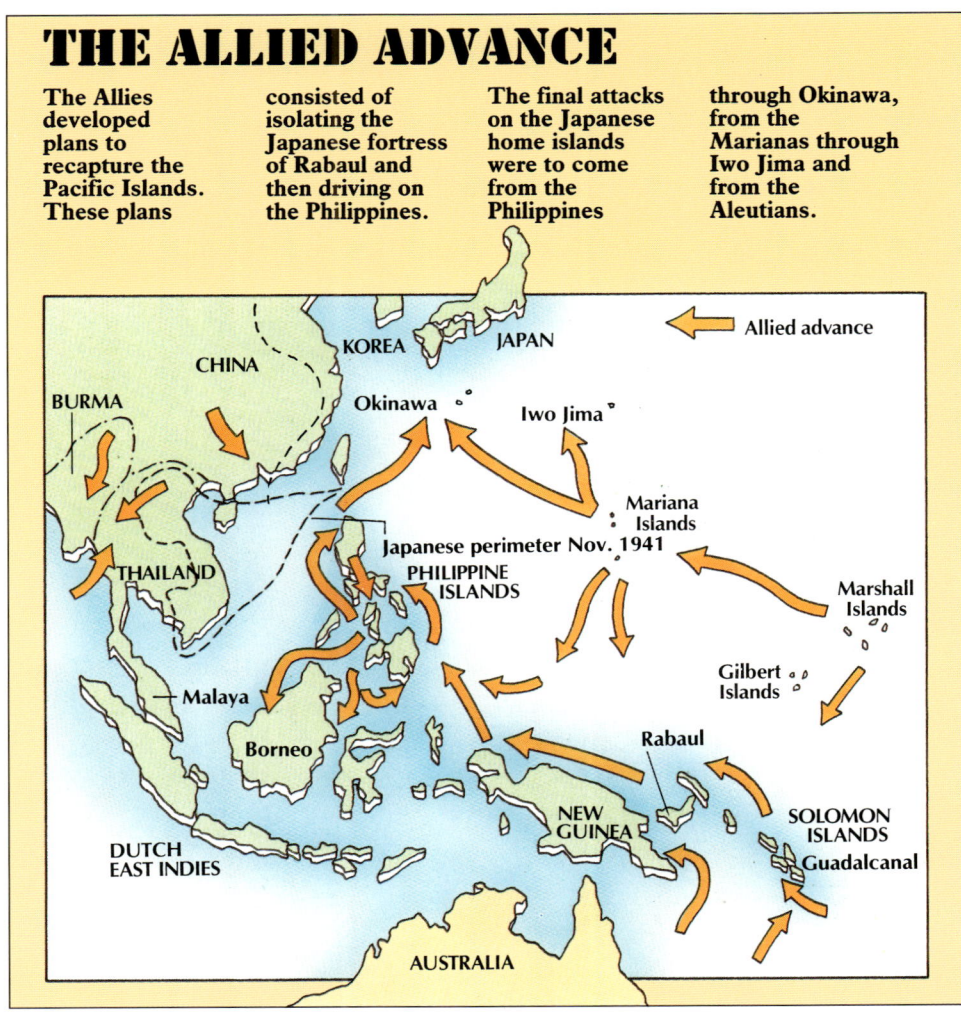

THE ALLIED ADVANCE

The Allies developed plans to recapture the Pacific Islands. These plans consisted of isolating the Japanese fortress of Rabaul and then driving on the Philippines. The final attacks on the Japanese home islands were to come from the Philippines through Okinawa, from the Marianas through Iwo Jima and from the Aleutians.

across the ocean were seized by Allied forces, while the major Japanese bases were bypassed, isolated and left to "wither on the vine". But as they approached the Japanese home islands, the Allies encountered fanatical resistance. It was anticipated that it might take another 18 months of fighting to overcome Japan. At the time of Yalta the development of the atomic bomb by the Americans was well advanced, but its power was as yet unknown. The amphibious assault on the island fortress of Iwo Jima, one of the last great hurdles before Japan itself, was in preparation but had not yet been launched.

The strategic bombing campaign against Japan, mounted from airstrips on the Marianas, was still

A coral reef is dynamited to provide a landing place for US supply ships during the fight for the island of Okinawa. This island was the scene of one of the grimmest of all the battles in the Pacific war. US Army and Marine dead amounted to nearly 7,000 and the Japanese defenders lost 110,000. As many as 150,000 Japanese civilians also died. The last pockets of Japanese resistance were mopped up at the end of May 1945.

THE MANHATTAN PROJECT

"The Manhattan Project" was the code-name for the development of the atomic bomb. The potential power of a nuclear reaction had been the subject of research by a number of physicists in the pre-war years. In January 1939 some of these scientists met in Washington DC to discuss the possibility of an atomic explosive.

The British and the Americans launched a research project to develop an atomic weapon. On 16 July 1945 the first bomb was successfully tested at Alamogordo, New Mexico. On 6 August 1945 the B-29 Superfortress bomber "Enola Gay" dropped the "Little Boy" atomic bomb on the Japanese city of Hiroshima, killing 78,000 people. Three days later another B-29 dropped the "Fat Man" bomb on Nagasaki, where 35,000 died. Japan surrendered on 15 August.

Hiroshima was devastated after the dropping of the atomic bomb, as shown above. President Harry Truman's decision to use the bomb was heavily influenced by estimates that an amphibious invasion of Japan might cost up to a million casualties. Another important factor was his desire to demonstrate US military might to the Soviet Union – which did not possess the bomb – as the war drew to a close.

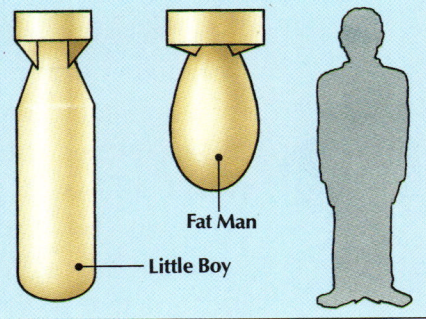

Fat Man

Little Boy

gathering strength. As a result, Roosevelt and his military advisers were eager to secure the Soviet Union's early entry into the war against Japan, which had over a million well-trained and armed troops tied down in Manchuria.

In pursuit of this goal, Roosevelt was prepared to make important concessions to Stalin over the future of Eastern Europe, which was now under the military control of the Red Army. Together they thwarted Churchill's attempts to tie down the future of post-war Europe. Instead, the Americans produced a "Declaration on Liberated Europe", a well-meaning but ambiguous document, among the provisions of which was the right of all peoples to choose the form of government under which they wished to live. This meant nothing to Stalin who was determined, above all, to ensure that Poland, the traditional invasion route into the Soviet Union, would remain firmly under Soviet control. As he bluntly put it, "Everyone imposes his own system as far as his army can reach. It cannot be otherwise." In return for a pledge to enter the war against Japan, Roosevelt was prepared to allow Stalin his way over Poland. Churchill was left out of the deal; the Soviet Union and the United States were the new superpowers.

Suspicious of Churchill's old-fashioned imperialist notions, and determined to limit the mischief-making capacity of the European states by assigning the Soviet Union a greater role in world affairs, Roosevelt helped set the shape of post-war Eastern Europe along the harsh lines which it has taken nearly 50 years to change. He did not live to see the result. On his return to the

United States he was clearly exhausted. On 12 April 1945, while resting at the clinic for the disabled he had established at Warm Springs, he died of a massive cerebral haemorrhage. Twenty-six days later the people of Europe celebrated VE (Victory in Europe) Day.

Roosevelt was succeeded by his vice president, Harry Truman. In July 1945 Truman attended the last big conference of the war at Potsdam. While returning from the conference, Truman announced his decision to drop an atomic bomb on Hiroshima in order to bring a speedy end to the war in the Far East.

Roosevelt had become president of the United States at one of the lowest points in its history. He left behind him the first global superpower, soon to be possessed of a nuclear arsenal. For better, and for worse, the topography of the modern world owes much to Roosevelt's guiding hand.

Roosevelt's funeral in 1945 was held in Washington DC. FDR was mourned by many Americans.

CHRONOLOGY

1882 Franklin Delano Roosevelt (FDR) born on the Springwood estate, New York.

1896 FDR enters Groton College, Massachusetts.

1900 FDR enters Harvard University; FDR's cousin, Theodore Roosevelt, is elected US vice president.

1901 September, Theodore Roosevelt succeeds to the presidency after the assassination of William McKinley.

1905 FDR marries Eleanor Roosevelt.

1910 FDR elected as a New York state senator.

1912 Woodrow Wilson elected US president.

1913 FDR appointed Assistant Secretary of the Navy.

1914 August, outbreak of World War I.

1917 April, the United States enters World War I.

1918 July, FDR makes a tour of the Western Front; 11 November, the armistice is signed.

1920 FDR nominated as Democratic candidate for US vice presidency.

1921 August, FDR is stricken with poliomyelitis.

1924 FDR delivers the nomination speech for Al Smith at the Democratic Convention.

1927 FDR establishes the Warm Springs Foundation for the care of polio victims.

1928 FDR elected governor of New York.

1932 FDR secures the nomination as Democratic candidate for the US presidency.

1933 January, Adolf Hitler appointed chancellor of Germany; March, FDR takes office as president; the Nazi Party confirmed in power in Germany by general election.

1936 FDR runs for re-election as US president and wins by a landslide.

1937 July, fighting between Japanese and Chinese troops near Peking marks start of Sino-Japanese war.

1938 September, Munich conference to resolve the Czech crisis.

1939 March, Czechoslovakia dismembered; September, Germany invades Poland, and Britain, France, Canada, South Africa, Australia and New Zealand declare war on Germany; United States proclaims neutrality in European war; November, "cash and carry" clause introduced in US Neutrality Act to permit Britain and France to buy arms.

1940 September, United States agrees to supply Britain with 50 destroyers in return for bases; FDR secures a third term as US president.

1941 March, FDR signs the Lend-Lease Act; July/August, FDR freezes Japanese assets in the United States and declares US oil embargo against "aggressors"; FDR meets Winston Churchill at Placentia Bay, Newfoundland and they issue the Atlantic Charter, the seed of the United Nations; 7 December, Japanese attack on Pearl Harbor; the United States enters World War II.

1942 May, Battle of the Coral Sea; June, Battle of Midway; August; US troops land on Guadalcanal.

1943 January, Churchill and FDR meet at Casablanca; May, Churchill and FDR meet in Washington DC to discuss plans for the invasion of France; August, Churchill and FDR meet in Quebec; November, Teheran conference marks the first summit between the "Big Three" (Churchill, FDR and Stalin).

1944 June, Allies invade Normandy; September, Churchill and FDR meet for the second time at Quebec, they agree to start work on a permanent United Nations Organization; FDR secures fourth term as US president.

1945 February, the "Big Three" meet at Yalta; Stalin agrees to enter the war in the Far East; 12 April, death of FDR; he is succeeded by Vice President Truman; May, unconditional surrender of all German forces to the Allies; 6 August, first atomic bomb dropped on Hiroshima; 9 August, second atomic bomb dropped; 15 August, Japan accepts Allied surrender terms.

GLOSSARY

Allies the nations fighting Germany, Italy and Japan during World War II. They included, from 1939, Great Britain (its empire and dominions), France (until 1940), the Soviet Union (from 1941), China and the United States (after December 1941).

Axis the powers allied to Germany during World War II – Italy (until 1943) and Japan.

Chief of Staff the most senior staff officer of an armed service.

Chief of the Imperial General Staff Chief of Staff of the armed forces of Great Britain.

Congress the law-making body of the United States. It consists of two houses: the Senate and the House of Representatives.

deficit financing an economic programme in which a government spends more money than it receives from taxes and other sources. It often indicates that the government is spending heavily on public works in order to stimulate an ailing economy.

Democratic Party one of the two main parties in the United States. With Roosevelt as a Democratic president, it stood for the people's interests and for government spending on public works and welfare.

division a number of regiments or battalions (usually 9-20,000 men) under the command of a major general.

governor the elected head of the state administration.

Great Depression the period of poverty and mass unemployment in the 1930s that resulted from the Wall Street Crash of 1929.

House of Representatives the lower house of Congress. The members of the House of Representatives are elected according to the size of the state's population.

isolationism a long-standing and powerful conviction held by many Americans that the United States' interests are best served by avoiding any foreign alliances or commitments which might damage the United States economically or lead to costly military ventures.

"New Deal" a general term that stems from Roosevelt's 1933 promise to provide the American people with "a new deal". The term is applied to the package of economic and political reforms undertaken by his administration between 1933 and 1940.

Republican Party one of the two main parties in the United States. Its members believe in restraining government expenditure and protecting state rights.

Senate one of the houses of Congress. In the Senate, each state, regardless of its size, is represented by two senators.

strategic bombing air attacks intended to influence the overall course of a war by interrupting the enemy's manufacture of armaments, destroying raw materials, disrupting transport, and undermining civilian morale.

U-boat German submarine.

Wall Street Crash the collapse of the New York stock exchange in October 1929. It led to a worldwide economic depression and mass unemployment.

FURTHER READING

Burns, J M *Roosevelt: The Lion and the Fox*, Harcourt, Brace, Jovanovich, 1958 *The Soldier of Freedom*, Harcourt, Brace, Jovanovich, 1970

Cole, W S *Roosevelt and the Isolationists, 1932-1945*, University of Nebraska Press, 1983

Hearden, P J *Roosevelt Confronts Hitler: America's Entry into World War II*, N. Illinois University Press, 1987

Keegan, J *The Second World War*, Hutchison, 1989

Lewin, R *The American Magic: Codes, Ciphers and the Defeat of Japan*, Farrar, Strauss and Giroux, 1982

Morgan T *FDR*, Grafton, 1986

Sargent, J *Roosevelt and the Hundred Days: Struggle for the Early New Deal*, New York: Garland Pub., 1981

INDEX

Photographic Credits:
Cover and pages 8, 19, 31, 39, 54 and 55: Popperfoto; pages 4, 21, 24, 27, 36, 44 and 47: Topham Picture Library; pages 12, 16, 22 and 25: Bettman Archives; pages 34, 49 and 52: Rex Features; pages 48 and 57: Hulton Picture Company.